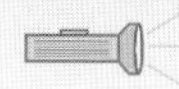

Tools Search Notes Discuss

MyReportLinks.com Books

Go!

 THE AMERICAN CIVIL WAR 

Reconstruction and Aftermath of the Civil War

A MyReportLinks.com Book

Lisa Harkrader

MyReportLinks.com Books
an imprint of

Enslow Publishers, Inc.

Box 398, 40 Industrial Road
Berkeley Heights, NJ 07922
USA

MyReportLinks.com Books, an imprint of Enslow Publishers, Inc. MyReportLinks® is a registered trademark of Enslow Publishers, Inc.

Library of Congress Cataloging-in-Publication Data

Harkrader, Lisa.
Reconstruction and aftermath of the Civil War / Lisa Harkrader.
v. cm. — (The American Civil War)
Includes bibliographical references and index.
Contents: The end of the war — Reconstruction : the first steps — President Johnson and the radical Republicans — Congressional reconstruction — African Americans after the war — An incomplete emancipation.
ISBN 0-7660-5265-6
1. Reconstruction—Juvenile literature. 2. United States—History—Civil War, 1861-1865—Influence—Juvenile literature. 3. United States—History—1865-1898—Juvenile literature. 4. African Americans—History—1863-1877—Juvenile literature. 5. African Americans—History—1877-1964—Juvenile literature. 6. Southern States—History—1865-1951—Juvenile literature. [1. Reconstruction—Juvenile literature. 2. United States—History—1865-1898. 3. African Americans—History—1863-1877—Sources. 4. Southern States—History—1865-1951.] I. Title. II. American Civil War (Berkeley Heights, N.J.)
E668.H28 2004
973.8—dc22
2003027541

Printed in the United States of America

10 9 8 7 6 5 4 3 2 1

To Our Readers:
Through the purchase of this book, you and your library gain access to the Report Links that specifically back up this book.
The Publisher will provide access to the Report Links that back up this book and will keep these Report Links up to date on **www.myreportlinks.com** for three years from the book's first publication date.
We have done our best to make sure all Internet addresses in this book were active and appropriate when we went to press. However, the author and the Publisher have no control over, and assume no liability for, the material available on those Internet sites or on other Web sites they may link to.
The usage of the MyReportLinks.com Books Web site is subject to the terms and conditions stated on the Usage Policy Statement on **www.myreportlinks.com**.
A password may be required to access the Report Links that back up this book. The password is found on the bottom of page 4 of this book.
Any comments or suggestions can be sent by e-mail to comments@myreportlinks.com or to the address on the back cover.

Photo Credits: © Hemera Technologies, Inc., 1997–2001, p. 9; Digital History, pp. 17, 23, 25, 29, 38; Library of Congress, pp. 1, 3, 11, 13, 15, 19, 21, 26, 31, 34, 37, 40, 42, 45; MyReportLinks.com Books, pp. 4, back cover; White House Collection, Courtesy of White House Historical Association, p. 32.

Cover Photo: All images, Library of Congress.

Cover Description: "Heroes of the Colored Race" featuring Blanche K. Bruce, Frederick Douglass, and Hiram Rhoades Revels; Lincoln assassination.

Contents

MyReportLinks.com Books

Great Books, Great Links, Great for Research!

The Report Links listed on the following four pages can save you hours of research time by **instantly** bringing you to the best Web sites relating to your report topic.

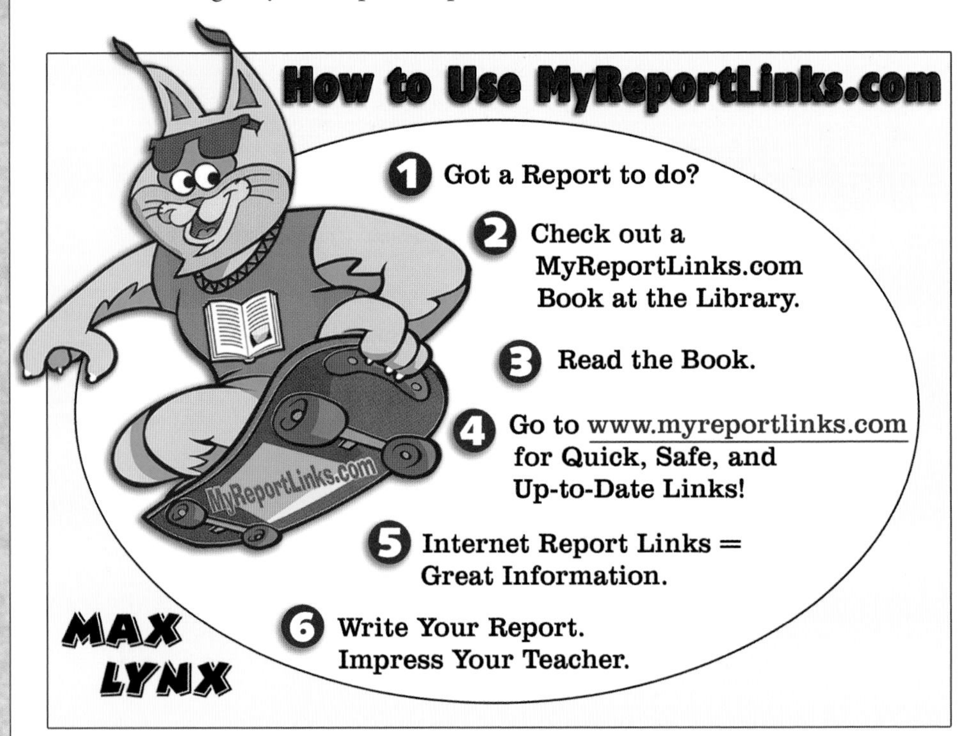

The pre-evaluated Web sites are your links to source documents, photographs, illustrations, and maps. They also provide links to dozens—even hundreds—of Web sites about your report subject.

MyReportLinks.com Books and the MyReportLinks.com Web site save you time and make report writing easier than ever!

Please see "To Our Readers" on the copyright page for important information about this book, the MyReportLinks.com Web site, and the Report Links that back up this book. Please enter **WRA4673** if asked for a password.

Report Links

The Internet sites described below can be accessed at http://www.myreportlinks.com

▶Reconstruction—The Second Civil War *EDITOR'S CHOICE

This PBS Reconstruction site covers topics such as the freeing of the slaves, the devastation of the South, the Freedmen's Bureau, the Ku Klux Klan, carpetbaggers, and more.

▶America's Reconstruction: People and Politics After the Civil War *EDITOR'S CHOICE

This Digital History site explores the post–Civil War period known as Reconstruction in depth. The text is illustrated with political documents, pamphlets, cartoons, photographs, memoirs, and more.

▶Civil War and Reconstruction, 1861–1877 *EDITOR'S CHOICE

Inside this Library of Congress Learning Page you will learn about the Civil War and Reconstruction. Photographs, documents, and interviews are all featured on this site.

▶America's Story from America's Library: Reconstruction (1866–1877) *EDITOR'S CHOICE

This Library of Congress site is dedicated to the Reconstruction era. Here you will find articles about such topics as the Andrew Johnson impeachment trial, the Fourteenth Amendment, and more.

▶Appomattox Court House *EDITOR'S CHOICE

Appomattox Court House is where Lee surrendered to Grant, bringing an end to the American Civil War. This National Park Service site contains information about the Battle of Appomattox, Lee's surrender, and this historic site.

▶CSS *Shenandoah* (1864–1865) *EDITOR'S CHOICE

James Iredell Waddell was the last Confederate officer to surrender during the Civil War. Here you can learn more about Waddell and his ship, the CSS *Shenandoah*.

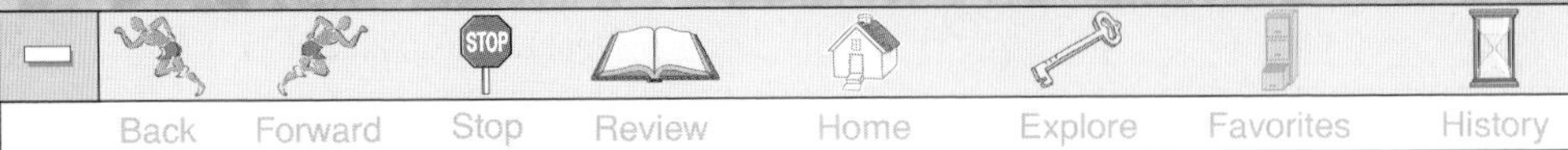

The Internet sites described below can be accessed at http://www.myreportlinks.com

▶African-American Odyssey

This Library of Congress page provides links to its sites related to the struggle for black Americans to gain citizenship. Here you will find Frederick Douglass's papers, slave narratives, and much more.

▶African American World: Ku Klux Klan

The Ku Klux Klan (KKK) is a white supremacist and terrorist organization that was formed during Reconstruction. Here you will find an overview of the Klan and its history.

▶African Americans in Congress: The Honorable Hiram Rhoades Revels

Here you will find a brief biography of Hiram Rhoades Revels. Revels became the first African-American man to serve in the United States Senate when he replaced Jefferson Davis, the former president of the Confederacy.

▶American Experience: Ulysses S. Grant

This PBS site on Ulysses S. Grant contains information focusing on his military and presidential years. His complete memoirs are also provided.

▶Andrew Johnson (1865–1869)

Andrew Johnson became president following Abraham Lincoln's assassination. Here you will learn about Johnson's theories on Reconstruction, his battle against impeachment, and more.

▶Assassination of President Abraham Lincoln

This Library of Congress site tells the story of President Abraham Lincoln's assassination by John Wilkes Booth in 1865.

▶Blanche Kelso Bruce, United States Senator: An Untold Story of Hannibal

Blanche Kelso Bruce taught at the Freedmen's Bureau's first school for ex-slaves. He later became a United States senator. This site includes a brief biography.

▶Bureau of Refugees, Freedmen, and Abandoned Lands

This University of Virginia site is about the work of the Freedmen's Bureau. Inside you will find newspaper articles, documents, and other resources.

Report Links

The Internet sites described below can be accessed at http://www.myreportlinks.com

▶Civil Rights: A Chronology

This time line from the Civil Rights Coalition for the 21st Century offers a brief history of the struggle for freedom and equality in America. The text links to helpful resources.

▶Documenting the American South

This University of North Carolina site contains hundreds of resources about Reconstruction. First-person narratives, literature, and documents can all be found here.

▶Finding Precedent: Hayes vs. Tilden

This site covers the 1876 presidential election and its controversial result, which was resolved by the Compromise of 1877.

▶Finding Precedent: The Impeachment of Andrew Johnson

This site features *Harper's Weekly* news, editorials, illustrations, and political cartoons that relate to the impeachment of President Andrew Johnson.

▶Freedmen's Bureau

Learn about the establishment and history of the Freedmen's Bureau, a government agency set up after the Civil War to provide short-term relief, including basic shelter and medical care, to former slaves and poor white Southerners.

▶The History of Jim Crow

The History of Jim Crow tells the story of segregation in America from its roots to the victories of the civil rights movement. In-depth history, essays, literature, narratives, and other resources are included here.

▶NAACP.org

The official site of the National Association for the Advancement of Colored People (NAACP) contains information about the history and current events of the organization.

▶The Papers of Jefferson Davis

This in-depth site contains the papers of Jefferson Davis. Check the Davis FAQs and Chronology to learn more about his trial for treason.

Report Links

The Internet sites described below can be accessed at http://www.myreportlinks.com

▶Pinckney Benton Stewart Pinchback

Pinckney Benton Stewart Pinchback was the first African-American governor in the history of the United States. Here you will find his biography.

▶President Abraham Lincoln's Second Inaugural Address (1865)

Lincoln's Second Inaugural Address is one of the most important speeches in the history of the United States. Lincoln's handwritten draft, a transcription, and background on the speech are also included.

▶Rainey, Joseph Hayne (1832–1887)

Joseph Hayne Rainey was the first African American to serve in the United States House of Representatives. This site presents a biography of Representative Rainey.

▶The Rise and Fall of Jim Crow

This interactive PBS site examines the story of the Jim Crow laws that discriminated against African Americans in the South following the Civil War. A time line contains events that occurred from 1863 to 1954.

▶Robert Smalls—1839–1915

Civil War hero Robert Smalls was the first African-American captain of a United States vessel and one of the first African-American senators. Here you will learn about his life and work.

▶Rutherford B. Hayes

On the official White House Web site, you can read a biography of President Rutherford B. Hayes, whose election in 1876 followed an election controversy.

▶Towards Racial Equality: *Harper's Weekly* Reports on Black America, 1857–1874

Here you will find *Harper's Weekly* editorials, news stories, illustrations, and political cartoons related to slavery, the Civil War, and Reconstruction.

▶*World Book*: The African American Journey

World Book's African American Journey charts the African-Americans experience and struggle for freedom from slavery to the modern civil rights movement.

Reconstruction and Aftermath of the Civil War Time Line

1865—*March:* Lincoln is sworn in for second term; the Bureau of Refugees, Freedmen, and Abandoned Lands is established temporarily.

April 9: Surrender of Lee to Grant at Appomattox Court House.

May 26: Johnson announces his Presidential Reconstruction plans, which offer amnesty to most Confederates.

December 6: Thirteenth Amendment is ratified; it prohibits slavery everywhere in the United States.

1866—*January:* Congress passes bill to extend Freedmen's Bureau and protect African Americans from Black Codes.

April: Congress, overriding a presidential veto, passes the Civil Rights Act of 1866.

Summer: Violence against African Americans erupts in the South.

1867—*March–July:* Congress passes three Reconstruction Acts, which divide most of the South into military districts.

1868—*March–May:* The House of Representatives votes to impeach Andrew Johnson. The Senate falls one vote short of removing him from office.

June–July: Arkansas, Louisiana, Florida, North Carolina, and South Carolina are readmitted to the Union. The Freedmen's Bureau ceases operations.

July 28: The Fourteenth Amendment is ratified.

November: Ulysses S. Grant is elected president; seven of the former Confederate states have been readmitted to the Union.

1869–1870—Redeemer governments are elected throughout the South.

1870—*January–March:* Virginia, Texas, and Mississippi are readmitted to the Union.

February 3: The Fifteenth Amendment, which guarantees voting rights regardless of race, is ratified.

July 1870: Georgia becomes the last Confederate state to be readmitted to the Union.

1870 and 1871—Grant signs Enforcement Acts and Ku Klux Klan Act.

1872—*November:* Grant is reelected president.

1874—*Fall:* Democrats win control of Congress, and redeemer governments continue in the South.

1875—*March:* Congress enacts the Civil Rights Act of 1875, which outlaws segregation.

1877—*February:* Contested presidential election of 1876 leads to the Compromise of 1877. Rutherford B. Hayes wins the presidency by agreement to end Reconstruction.

Chapter 1

The End of the War

On April 9, 1865, Confederate general Robert E. Lee surrendered his Army of Northern Virginia to Union general Ulysses S. Grant in the village of Appomattox Court House, Virginia. Lee's surrender ended the American Civil War, four years of the bloodiest fighting the United States has ever seen. More than 620,000 soldiers lost their lives, and almost 400,000 were wounded. But soldiers were not the only casualties of war: About fifty thousand Confederate civilians were killed.

Terms of Surrender

General Grant saw how devastating the war had been for Southerners, and he also had great respect for General Lee. Grant and Lee had served together in the United States Army before the Southern states seceded from, or left, the Union. General Grant's terms of surrender were generous. Confederate soldiers would not be taken prisoners of war. They were free to return to their homes and allowed to take their mules and horses home with them. It was planting season, and Grant knew that without horses or mules, Southern farmers would not be able to plant or harvest their crops.

Lee's army had run out of rations. For days, the soldiers had eaten nothing but parched corn. Grant ordered his men to give them food. He also stopped his Union soldiers from firing a one-hundred-gun salute to celebrate their victory. General Grant knew the Confederate

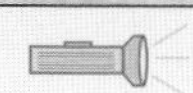
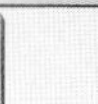

soldiers would hear them. "The Confederates were now our prisoners, and we did not want to exult over their downfall," he wrote.[1]

The End of the Fighting

When Robert E. Lee surrendered to Ulysses S. Grant, he did not surrender the entire Confederacy. He only surrendered the troops under his command.

A lithograph portrays the surrender of Confederate general Robert E. Lee to Union general Ulysses S. Grant at Appomattox Court House on April 9, 1865. The end of the war marked the beginning of Reconstruction.

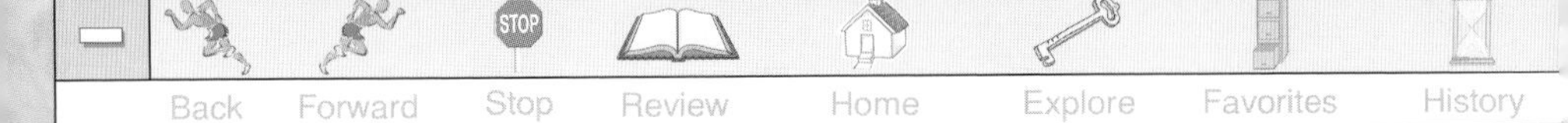

But both Northerners and Southerners knew the war was over. General Lee was the South's greatest military leader. The South could not win without Lee and his army. On April 26, Confederate General Joseph Johnston surrendered his army to Union General William Tecumseh Sherman in North Carolina. On May 4, Confederate General Richard Taylor, the son of former United States president Zachary Taylor, surrendered his army to Union forces in Alabama.

But some Confederate troops continued to fight. A month after Lee's surrender, Confederate soldiers still held territory near Brownsville, Texas. On May 12, Union forces tried to capture these soldiers, but the Confederates drove the Union troops away. The Battle at Palmito Ranch was the last land battle of the Civil War. The Confederates held out for two more weeks until news of Lee's surrender finally reached them.

Confederate General E. Kirby Smith commanded the Trans-Mississippi Department, the Confederate army west of the Mississippi River. Smith did not want to surrender, but he and his officers realized they could not fight the war alone. On May 26, General Smith surrendered his army in New Orleans.

Confederate General Stand Watie, a Cherokee leader, commanded a small group of American Indian troops in what is now Oklahoma. General Watie knew the Confederacy was doomed, but he refused to give up. He held out until June 23, when he finally surrendered to Union troops. Stand Watie was the last Confederate general to surrender.

The End of the Confederacy

Nine days before Lee surrendered, Union troops advanced on Richmond, Virginia, which was the Confederate capital. Jefferson Davis, the president of the Confederacy, fled with other Confederate officials. They planned to reestablish their government in Texas.

A month later, on May 10, Union troops captured Davis in Georgia. The United States government charged him with treason. Davis spent two years in jail. Northern newspaper editor Horace Greeley finally raised money for Davis's bail. Greeley strongly opposed slavery, but he hoped to heal the wounds between the North and the South.

Davis went to Canada to await his trial for treason, but the trial never came. In the years after the war, most Northerners lost interest in punishing Confederate leaders. They knew that bringing Davis to trial would only deepen the divide between North and South. On Christmas Day 1868, President Andrew Johnson granted amnesty to all former Confederate leaders.

Jefferson Davis, who had served as president of the Confederate States of America, was released on bail provided by one of the North's most ardent supporters—Horace Greeley, publisher of the New York Tribune.

The Ravaged South

Nearly all of the fighting in the Civil War had taken place in the South. Toward the end of the war, Union troops under General Sherman marched from Atlanta to Savannah, Georgia, on the Atlantic coast. This military action became known as "Sherman's march to the sea." Along the way, the troops burned cities, houses, farms, railroads, and factories. They destroyed almost everything in their path. General Sherman believed that the sooner he brought the South to its knees, the sooner the war would end.

Four months later, the war was over, and the South lay in ruins. Thousands of Southerners were homeless. They had little food, their fields were burned, and their Confederate money was worthless. Confederate soldiers choked the roads, trying to make their way home. Four million slaves were now free. Many of these former slaves, now called freedmen, wandered the South, looking for lost relatives and a new way of life. That new way of life would be hard won, however.

Chapter 2

Reconstruction: The First Steps

During the last two years of the war, Northern troops captured many areas of the South. By December 1863, Union troops occupied Tennessee, most of North Carolina and Louisiana, and parts of other Confederate states. The Union also controlled the Mississippi River. President Abraham Lincoln began making plans for Reconstruction, a plan to bring the Confederate states back into the Union and heal the nation's wounds.

Lincoln's Plan

Throughout the war, Lincoln's main goal had been to restore the Union—to make the United States one country again. He did not want to make it difficult or painful for

The rebuilding of the South and the reentry of Southern states into the Union was just one of the many tasks that lay ahead during Reconstruction.

Southern states to reenter the Union. On December 8, 1863, Lincoln announced his first plan for Reconstruction. Under this plan, Confederate states controlled by Union troops would be able to rejoin the United States.

Lincoln's Reconstruction plan allowed all white Southerners, except Confederate leaders, to become American citizens again by taking an oath. In this oath, they would swear to be loyal to the United States. When 10 percent of the voters in a Confederate state who had voted in 1860 had taken the oath, that state could send representatives to Congress. The state would once again be part of the Union. Lincoln also required each state to abolish slavery.

Lincoln's Ten Percent Plan angered many Northerners, including some congressmen. These congressmen thought Lincoln was being too easy on the South. They were furious that the Southern states had seceded from the Union and waged war on the North. They were outraged that thousands of Union soldiers had died. In 1864, Congress wrote its own Reconstruction bill, the Wade-Davis Bill. This bill required half of a state's voters who had voted in 1860 to swear loyalty before the state could rejoin the Union. Lincoln thought the bill was too harsh and would not sign it. Without his signature and with fewer than ten days left in the congressional session, the bill was automatically vetoed.

On March 4, 1865, Lincoln took the oath of office for his second presidential term. In his second inaugural address, he spoke against slavery. But he showed compassion for the Southern states, saying, "Let us judge not that we be not judged."[1] He ended the speech with these famous words:

With malice toward none; with charity for all; with firmness in the right, as God gives us to see the right, let us strive on to finish the work we are in; to bind up the nation's wounds; to care for him who shall have borne the battle, and for his widow, and his orphan—to do all which may achieve and cherish a just, and a lasting peace, among ourselves, and with all nations.[2]

The Freedmen's Bureau

In March 1865, a month before the end of the war, Congress created the Bureau of Refugees, Freedmen, and

The Freedmen's Bureau was Congress' attempt to provide help to former slaves during Reconstruction. But even at its peak, the bureau employed only nine hundred agents in the South to try to accomplish what was a monumental task.

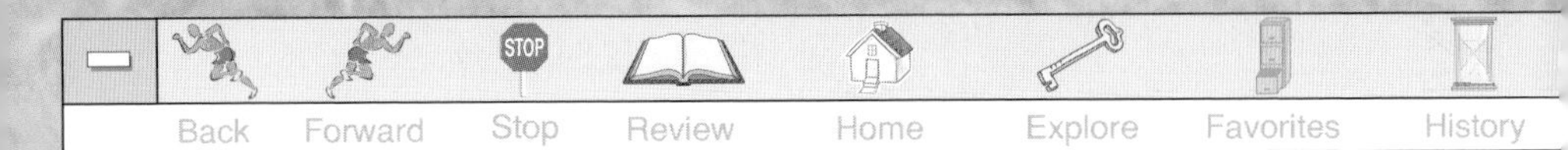

Abandoned Lands. This agency became known as the Freedmen's Bureau. Its mission was to help former slaves establish lives as free people.

Congress appointed General Oliver Otis Howard to head the Freedmen's Bureau. General Howard, who had served in the Union army, strongly opposed slavery and was truly concerned about the plight of African Americans. The Freedmen's Bureau set up offices all over the South. Under General Howard's command, these offices furnished millions of dollars of food, clothing, and medicine to freedmen, or former slaves. The Freedmen's Bureau also helped poor whites who had become homeless and destitute because of the war.

Southern African Americans were no longer slaves. But they had to earn a living. Many of them went to work for their former masters, the plantation owners. Since most freedmen could not read, the Freedmen's Bureau approved labor contracts between freedmen and plantation owners to keep the plantation owners from taking unfair advantage of the freedmen.

The Freedmen's Bureau also built forty hospitals and thousands of schools for African Americans. At first, teachers from the North volunteered to teach in the schools. The bureau then began training African-American teachers. Freedmen of all ages flocked to the schools, eager to finally get an education. The Freedmen's Bureau helped establish colleges for African Americans, such as Fisk, Atlanta, and Howard universities and the Hampton Institute.

Forty Acres and a Mule

The Freedmen's Bureau controlled over 800,000 acres of land in the South. The Union had confiscated much of this land from Confederate plantation owners, and Southern landowners had also abandoned some of the land during the war.

Toward the end of the war, the Union allowed freedmen to farm some of this abandoned land. As General Sherman's army marched toward the sea, it freed slaves along the way. These newly freed slaves had no way to make a living, so they began following the Union army, hoping the soldiers would feed them. General Sherman issued wartime orders to provide the freedmen with farmland so that they would be able to support themselves. He set aside confiscated lands in Mississippi, Florida, and the islands off the coast of South Carolina and Georgia. He ordered his officers to allow each African-American family to farm not more than forty acres of this land. He also allowed the army to lend African-American families farm animals that the army could no longer use.

When Congress created the Freedmen's Bureau, it also gave General Howard the authority to lease "not more than forty acres of such land" to freedmen.[3] General Howard planned to divide the abandoned land into forty-acre plots. He would distribute the plots to former slaves to farm.

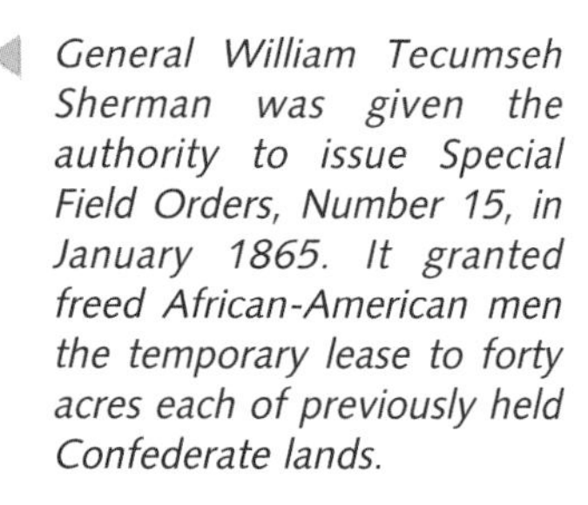

General William Tecumseh Sherman was given the authority to issue Special Field Orders, Number 15, in January 1865. It granted freed African-American men the temporary lease to forty acres each of previously held Confederate lands.

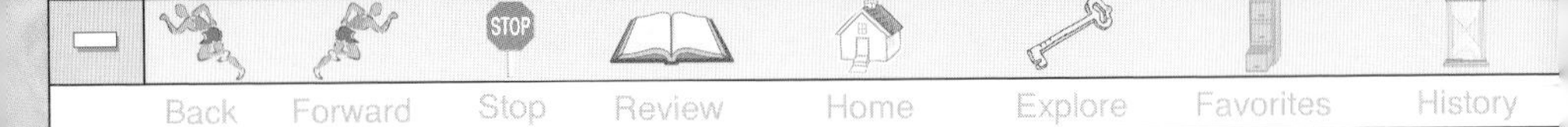

Freedmen believed that the government would soon give each of them "forty acres and a mule."

Lincoln's Assassination

On April 14, 1865, five days after Lee surrendered to Grant, President Lincoln attended the play *Our American Cousin* at Ford's Theatre in Washington, D.C.

Theatergoers wanted to get a glimpse of the president. An actor and Southern sympathizer named John Wilkes Booth was especially interested in Lincoln. In the last months of the war, Booth and a few friends had plotted to kidnap the president to force the release of Confederate prisoners of war. But with the war over, and prisoners released, Booth changed his plans.

A little after 10:00 P.M., Booth slipped into the president's box at the theater and shot Lincoln in the back of the head and then leaped from the box to the stage, breaking his leg in the fall. He hobbled from the theater and escaped on a waiting horse.

Soldiers carried the wounded president across the street to a boardinghouse. Abraham Lincoln never regained consciousness and died early the next morning.

John Wilkes Booth evaded police officers and Union troops for eleven days until April 26, when soldiers tracked him to a Virginia tobacco barn. When Booth refused to come out, the soldiers set fire to the barn. As the fire blazed, Booth was shot. Some people believe a soldier shot him, while others think Booth shot himself. However Booth died, one thing was evident: The nation would now have to try to heal and reunite without the man who had steered it through the Civil War.

Chapter 3 ▶

President Johnson and the Radical Republicans

John Wilkes Booth had done the South no favors when he assassinated President Lincoln. Booth believed he would be a hero to Southerners, who would admire him for striking a blow against the hated North.

There were, of course, Southerners who, like Booth, had considered Lincoln a tyrant and did not mourn the president's death. But Lincoln's assassination also horrified many Southerners who believed in the causes they had fought for during the war but did not believe in murder. Some Southerners thought Lincoln would have dealt fairly with the former Confederate states. Now that he was gone, their fate was in the hands of men who would not be as forgiving.

Lincoln's plans for Reconstruction would never be enacted.

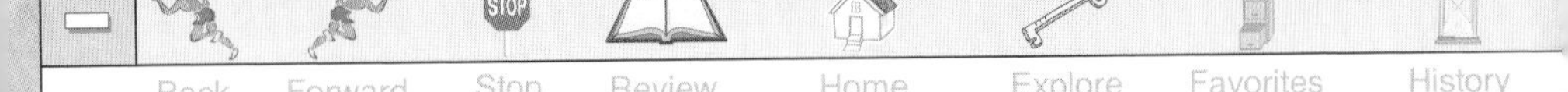

President Johnson

Andrew Johnson became vice president of the United States on March 4, 1865. Six weeks later, John Wilkes Booth shot Abraham Lincoln, and Johnson was then sworn in as president.

Johnson had grown up in a poor Southern family. He hated wealthy Southern plantation owners. It angered him that Southern aristocrats lived in luxury while poor whites barely made a living. Throughout his political career, he fought for the rights of working white people.

He was not as sympathetic toward slaves, however. Before the war, Johnson supported slavery. In fact, he owned a few slaves himself. During the war, he began to oppose slavery. But he still did not think African Americans should have the same rights that white Americans had.

Johnson believed strongly in the Union. Before the war, he had been a United States senator from Tennessee. When Southern states began talking about leaving the Union, Johnson gave a passionate speech before Congress. "It is treason, nothing but treason," he said of the South's plan to secede.[1] He desperately tried to keep his own state, Tennessee, from leaving the Union. But by 1861, eleven Southern states, including Tennessee, had seceded. Johnson was the only Southern senator who remained loyal to the United States.

The Radical Republicans

During and after the war, the Republican party, which was antislavery, controlled Congress. But one group of Republicans, called the Radicals, did not want to simply end slavery. They wanted to give black Americans equal rights with whites, including the right to vote. They wanted to change Southern society so that white Southerners could not discriminate against blacks. They did not want to make changes gradually, as some moderate Republicans recommended. Radical Republicans wanted these changes to come immediately.

Two of the most outspoken Radical Republican leaders were Charles Sumner and Thaddeus Stevens. Sumner was a senator from Massachusetts. Stevens was a representative from Pennsylvania. Both of these men had been staunch and vocal abolitionists throughout their political careers.

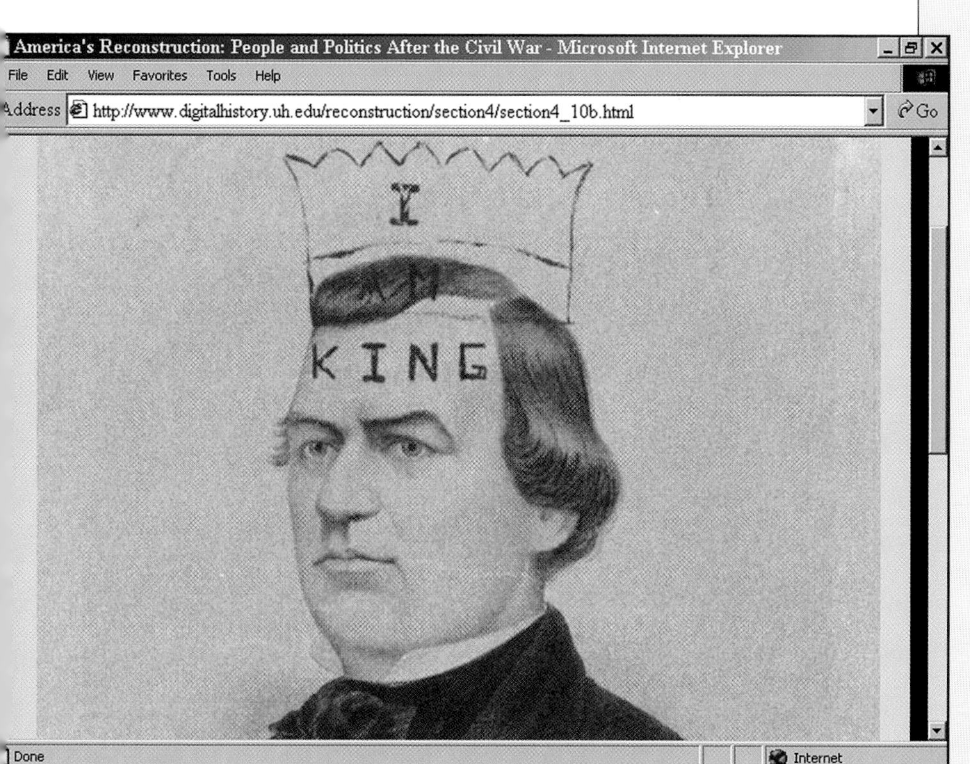

Andrew Johnson's constant battles with the Radical Republicans led many to consider him a tyrant. In this print in which he declares himself king, he is portrayed as less than democratic.

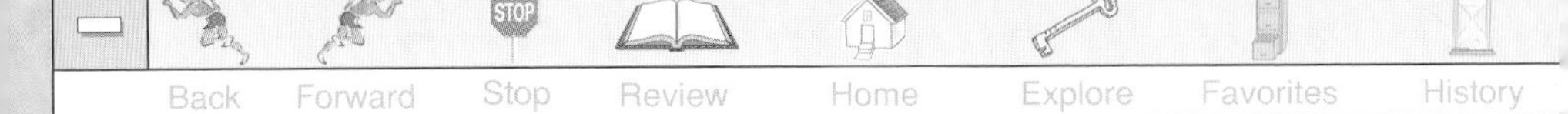

Radical Republicans believed that freedmen could not be equal with whites unless they had the same economic opportunities. Many Radicals, including Stevens, wanted the government to confiscate plantations owned by wealthy Southerners and divide this land among former slaves. This would accomplish two Radical Republican goals: It would punish former Confederates, and it would give freedmen a way to make a living.

Johnson's Reconstruction Plan

At first, the Radicals were thrilled that Andrew Johnson had become president. In the days following Lincoln's death, the country was in mourning, and emotions ran high. Johnson's emotions ran high, too. Though he said he had not yet developed a firm policy for Reconstruction, he also spoke several times of treason. "Treason is a crime," he said, "and must be punished."[2] Radicals believed Johnson was referring to the secession of the Southern states, and they thought Johnson wanted to punish the South as much as they did.

But Johnson was a Southerner. He believed that most of the people in the South had been led into rebellion by Southern plantation owners, but he did not want to tear the South apart. He wanted to rebuild the South by the time Congress returned to Washington in December. He believed a lenient Reconstruction policy would restore peace quickly. He did not want to make enemies of Southern voters.

On May 26, 1865, Johnson announced his Reconstruction plan. He offered amnesty to most former Confederates. If these Confederates took an oath of loyalty to the United States, they would once again be American citizens. Johnson's blanket pardon did not apply to a number of former Confederates. High-ranking Confederate military officers and government officials, as well as former Confederates who owned land worth at least $20,000, would be required to ask the president for individual pardons. Johnson eventually pardoned fourteen thousand high-ranking Confederates. He ordered the government to give back any land that had been confiscated from them.

Johnson appointed a temporary governor for each Southern state. Johnson's Reconstruction plan urged the

Freed slaves, now homeless, follow the Union army as it crosses the Rappahannock River in Virginia. The new responsibilities for African Americans in the South during Reconstruction meant they would have to find jobs and make a living without training or education.

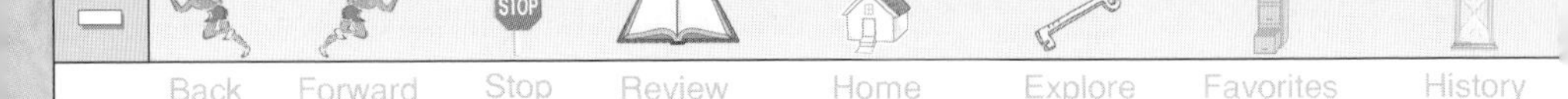

voters in each state to take the oath of loyalty to the United States, but it did not force them to do so. Each state also had to write a new state constitution and ratify, or pass, the Thirteenth Amendment, which abolished slavery. Johnson's plan did not give African Americans the right to vote, however. Johnson believed each state should decide for itself whether to allow African Americans to vote.

The Black Codes

Most Southern whites resented Northerners meddling in their government. They did not want former slaves to have equal rights with whites. As they formed their new state governments, Southern white politicians passed laws intended to keep freedmen as near slaves as they had been.

These laws were called the Black Codes. The Black Codes made sure that African Americans had few civil rights, few personal freedoms, and few options—but many responsibilities, such as providing for their families and finding employment.

An elderly African-American couple is photographed in their rural Virginia cabin in the late 1800s.

Plantation owners forced former slaves to sign work contracts. If they left their plantation job before the contract was up, they could be arrested. If they did not have a job, they could also be arrested. In some places, blacks could not hunt or fish. They could not own or rent land. They could not travel or enter towns without permission from their white employers. Blacks could not own guns. They could not assemble together, even at church, without permission. These laws made sure that African Americans could not earn a living in any way except as servants and field hands.

African Americans still lacked the rights that white Americans took for granted. Blacks could not vote. They could not hold public office or serve on juries. Blacks could not charge whites with crimes, even serious crimes such as assault and murder. But white authorities routinely arrested freedmen on flimsy charges. Blacks could be arrested for speaking disrespectfully toward a white person. They could be arrested for spending their own money in ways whites considered foolish. Southern prisons rented black prisoners to plantation owners as cheap labor. Many blacks were charged with being unfit parents. The state could then take their children and give them to plantation owners as apprentices, keeping these children as virtual slaves.

Congressional Reconstruction

Radical Republicans were outraged by President Johnson's lenient treatment of Southern states, but they were even more outraged at the Black Codes. Even moderate Republicans grew angry over the president's lack of concern for African Americans.

Congress convened again in December 1865. Southern states sent their senators and representatives. Many of these newly elected Southern congressmen had been staunch Confederates during the war, including Alexander H. Stephens, who had been the vice president of the Confederacy. Several others had been Confederate generals, and many had not taken the oath of loyalty.[1] Northern congressmen were furious and refused to seat the Southerners.

Congress Acts

In January 1866, Congress passed a bill to keep the Freedmen's Bureau alive and protect freedmen from the Black Codes. But President Johnson vetoed the bill.

The Republican congressmen were furious. They passed a Civil Rights Act that gave American citizenship to everyone born or naturalized in the United States, except American Indians. The act guaranteed African Americans equal civil rights. Johnson vetoed the act. But this time Congress had enough votes—a two-thirds majority—to override Johnson's veto, and the Civil Rights

Act became law. It was the first time that Congress had overridden the presidential veto of an important bill.

Republican congressmen were worried that when Southern congressmen finally took their seats in Congress, the Southerners would vote to repeal the Civil Rights Act. They also worried that the Supreme Court could rule the Civil Rights Act unconstitutional. In June 1866, Congress passed the Fourteenth Amendment to the U.S. Constitution. The Fourteenth Amendment reinforced the Civil Rights Act by guaranteeing citizenship to all people born or naturalized in the United States. It gave all citizens equal protection under the law. To become part

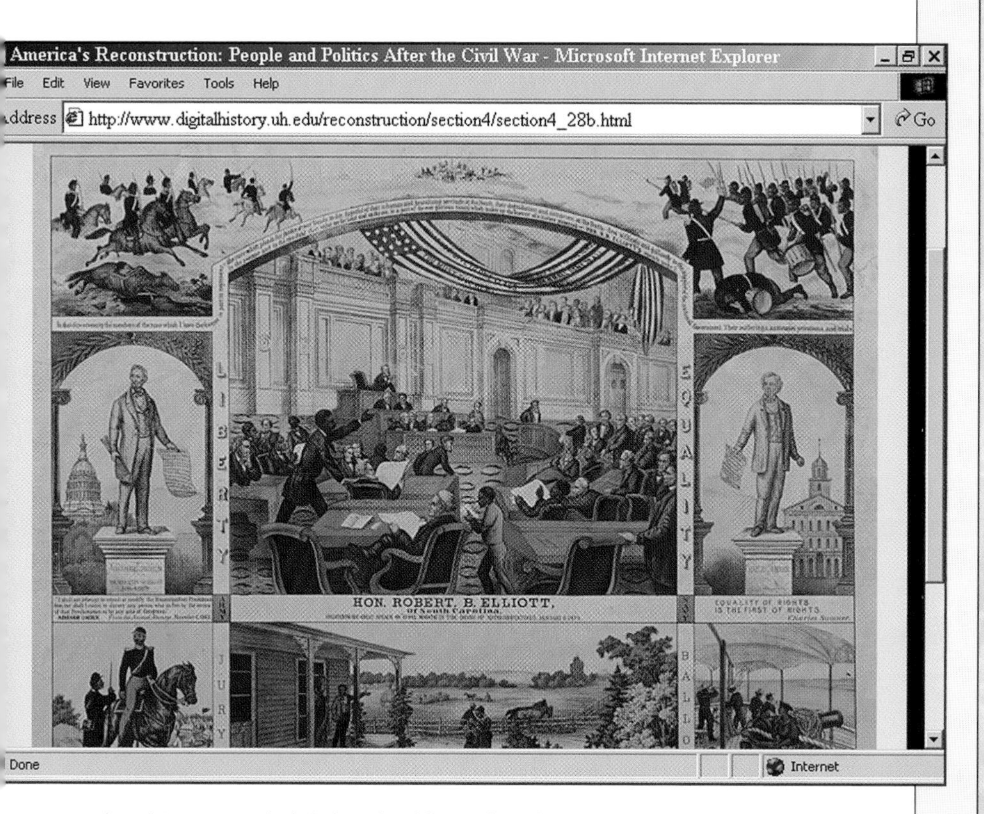

This print titled "The Shackle Broken by the Genius of Freedom" celebrates the history and heroes of African-American freedom.

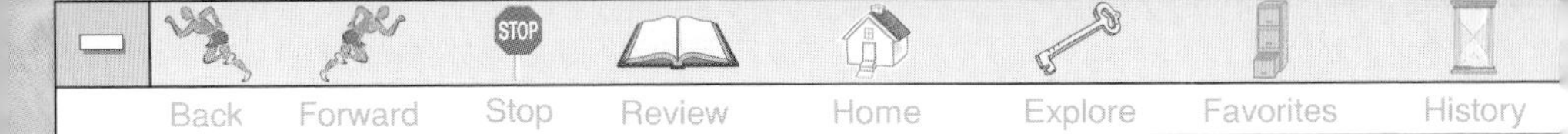

of the Constitution, the amendment had to be ratified, or approved, by three fourths of the states. Congress then passed another Freedmen's Bureau Bill. When Johnson vetoed the bill, Congress overrode that veto as well.

Not everyone in the North believed African Americans deserved equal rights with whites. Although most Northerners opposed slavery, many did not believe blacks were equal to whites, and many did not want blacks to vote. In many Northern states, blacks could *not* vote.

But now violence against African Americans erupted across the South. In May 1866, a white mob killed forty-six African Americans in Memphis, Tennessee. On July 30, 1866, thirty-seven blacks and three of their white supporters died in New Orleans when whites rioted over the black vote. White policemen led the riot.[2]

The Reconstruction Act of 1867

Northern voters were horrified by the violence. In congressional elections in November 1866, Northerners voted overwhelmingly for Republicans. Republican congressmen now had more power than ever. In March 1867, they passed their own Reconstruction Act. The act divided former Confederate states (except Tennessee, which had already ratified the Fourteenth Amendment) into five military districts. An army general governed each district. Congress stationed twenty thousand soldiers in the South to support the military governments.

This time, African Americans could vote, but former Confederates could not. Once a state ratified the Fourteenth Amendment and wrote a state constitution that guaranteed African Americans the right to vote, Congress would remove the military government. Johnson vetoed the Reconstruction Act, but Congress overrode his veto.

Johnson's Impeachment

President Johnson and the Republicans were locked in battle at every turn. Republicans, tired of dealing with Johnson, passed laws that limited the president's powers. One of these laws, the Tenure of Office Act, banned the president from removing members of his cabinet without the Senate's approval. Johnson, a strong supporter of the Constitution, did not believe that Congress had the power to take away the president's authority. In February 1868, Johnson deliberately defied the Tenure of Office Act by firing Edwin Stanton, the secretary of war.

The House of Representatives voted to impeach the president, or charge him with a crime. The Senate

"The Smelling Committee" satirizes the impeachment proceedings against Andrew Johnson by showing Radical Republican congressmen surrounding the rotting carcass of a horse (Andrew Johnson) that is wrapped in a blanket, representing impeachment.

The Union hero of the Civil War, Ulysses S. Grant seemed the antidote for Johnson's failings when Grant was elected president in November 1868. But continued violence against African Americans in the South, a depressed economy, and corruption in his own administration led to difficult terms in office for the general.

then tried Johnson. It held hearings to determine if Johnson was guilty. If two thirds of the Senate voted against him, Johnson would be removed from office.

But a few moderate Republican senators who were not sure that the Tenure of Office Act was constitutional worried that Congress was going too far. On May 16, 1868, the Senate voted thirty-five to nineteen to convict Johnson, but their vote fell one vote short of the two-thirds majority they needed. Andrew Johnson remained president for the rest of his term.

President Grant

In November 1868, General Ulysses S. Grant, the hero of the Union victory in the Civil War, was elected president. By that time, seven Confederate states had been readmitted to the Union. Only four—Georgia, Texas, Virginia, and Mississippi—remained under military occupation.

Grant's campaign slogan had been "Let us have peace," and Grant tried to follow through on that promise. He wanted to protect freedmen while dealing fairly with Southern whites. Grant successfully negotiated to readmit Georgia, Texas, Virginia, and Mississippi to the Union. He agreed that those states could allow former Confederates to vote. But he also required them to ratify the Fifteenth Amendment. This amendment guaranteed that "the right of citizens of the United States to vote shall not be denied or abridged by the United States or by any State on account of race, color, or previous condition of servitude."[3] The Fifteenth Amendment applied only to men, however.

At first, Grant wanted to limit the power of federal troops in the South. But he was appalled by the violent crimes that some Southern whites were committing against blacks. He sent federal troops to the South to stop white hate groups from terrorizing and killing blacks, and he urged Congress to pass bills to protect Southern blacks.

Grant was an honest man, but some of his advisers were not. Corruption and scandal plagued his two terms of office. Some members of his administration cheated the government out of tax money. His brother-in-law helped unscrupulous investors who wanted to illegally control the price of gold. The country was in economic peril as well. Banks collapsed, and workers lost their jobs. When Grant's second term of office ended, he did not run again.

President Hayes

In the 1876 presidential election, Democratic candidate Samuel J. Tilden won more popular votes than Republican candidate Rutherford B. Hayes, a former Union officer. But three Southern states—South Carolina, Florida, and Louisiana—turned in two sets of electoral ballots. One set gave Hayes the states' electoral votes. The other set gave some of the votes to Tilden. In Oregon, a Democratic elector was replaced by a Republican elector when it became

known that the Democrat held both a state and federal position, in violation of Oregon's constitution.

Democrats and Republicans battled over the election for several months. Congress appointed a commission to investigate the election. Finally, Democrats and Republicans struck a deal known as the Compromise of 1877. Republicans agreed to remove federal troops from Southern states and to spend money on improvements in the South. They also agreed to declare Reconstruction over. Southern Democrats then agreed to give Rutherford B. Hayes the presidency.

Southern politicians also promised to treat African Americans fairly. But many had no intention of keeping that promise. And by this time, many Northerners had grown tired of the problems in the South. Northerners believed that the Thirteenth, Fourteenth, and Fifteenth Amendments had given freedmen equal rights, and they turned their attention away from the South. With federal troops and Northerners no longer looking over their shoulders, Southern whites were free to once again pass laws that were unfair to Southern blacks.

Rutherford B. Hayes became president through a compromise that led to the end of Reconstruction.

Chapter 5 ▶

African Americans After the War

The Union victory in the American Civil War freed 4 million slaves. These freedmen now had to make lives for themselves when they had known nothing before but slavery. It had been illegal for slaves to learn to read, write, do arithmetic, or to get any other kind of formal education, so most freedmen were illiterate.

Some freedmen went North. Some went in search of parents, husbands, wives, or children who had been sold off during slavery. Some had no choice but to work for their former masters. They received low wages and toiled under unfair working conditions.

Sharecropping

Wealthy Southern landowners still wanted cheap farm labor. They replaced slavery with a system called sharecropping. Poor blacks and whites, called sharecroppers, rented small plots of land from plantation owners. As payment, the sharecropper gave part of his yearly crop to the landowner. The landowner lent sharecroppers money for seed, fertilizer, tools, food, and clothing, and in return, the sharecropper promised to pay for these things from the profit he made from his portion of the crop.

But sharecroppers seldom made a profit. When crops failed or when crop prices fell, the sharecropper could not pay what he owed, and many sharecroppers fell deeper and deeper into dept. They could not leave their rented

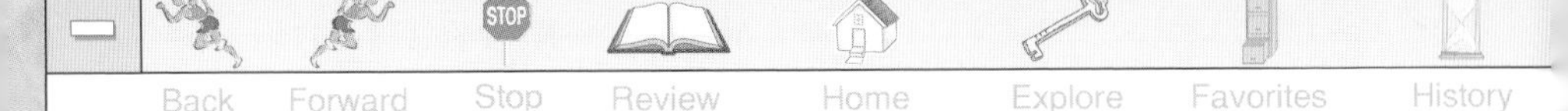

land until they paid what they owed to the landowner. Sharecroppers were hardly better off than slaves. Sharecropping continued in the South until well into the twentieth century.

Carpetbaggers and Scalawags

Southern landowners were not the only people to profit after the war. Thousands of Northerners moved south during Reconstruction. Southerners resented these Northerners and called them carpetbaggers because they carried their belongings in suitcases made of carpeting. Some carpetbaggers did profit from the chaos that existed in the South. Because of this, carpetbaggers earned the reputation of being dishonest and greedy.

But not all carpetbaggers had come to take advantage of Southerners. Many came to help the African Americans, often as part of the Freedmen's Bureau. Some came to teach in new black schools. Some came to help African Americans vote and run for political offices. Some came to run for political office themselves. Others wanted to invest in the South by building factories and businesses. Many carpetbaggers were Union army officers who decided to stay in the South after the war.

Not all Southern whites had agreed with the Confederacy during the war. Many were poor farmers who resented the wealthy plantation owners. They resented having to fight a war to help plantation owners keep their slaves. They had not wanted their states to secede from the Union. After the war, many of these Southern whites cooperated with carpetbaggers. They wanted to rebuild Southern society so that the plantation owners did not have more power and opportunities than poor people. Other Southerners referred to these

The stories of former slaves, including those of Sarah Gudger (pictured at age one hundred twenty-one), paint a picture of promises unfulfilled and lives that were not truly free, despite acts of Congress.

Southern whites as "scalawags" and considered them traitors to the South.

Voting

During Reconstruction, freedmen, carpetbaggers, and scalawags voted overwhelmingly for Republicans, so Republican governments dominated the Southern states. By 1870, a few African Americans had won elections for top government posts. Seventeen African-American men served in Congress. Others held important positions in state governments. They were among the first African Americans to hold office in the United States.

Many Southern whites claimed that black elected officials were ignorant and incompetent. They said Northerners were using these black officials as puppets who would do what the Northerners wanted. It was true that most African Americans in the South were illiterate at the time. But most of the blacks elected to Congress were educated men who took their positions seriously. They were often clergymen and teachers.

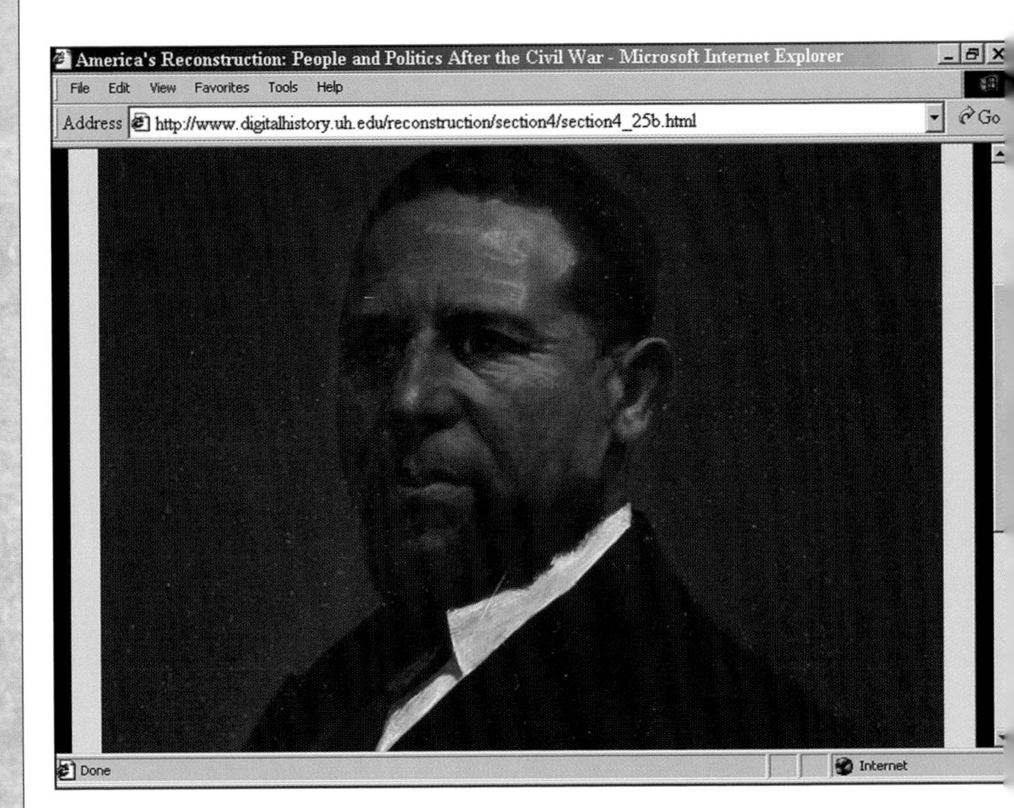

Hiram Revels, the first African American to serve in the United States Senate, is pictured. The abolitionist Frederick Douglass remarked on Revels' dignified image in this painting as an unusual portrayal, since African Americans were often depicted in unflattering ways.

African Americans in Government

Hiram Rhoades Revels was the first African American to serve in the United States Senate. He was a senator from Mississippi from 1870 to 1871. He was appointed to fill the Senate seat previously held by Jefferson Davis, former president of the Confederacy. Revels was a free black born in North Carolina. An ordained minister, he attended Knox College in Illinois. Before the Civil War, he was the principal of a black school in Maryland. During the war, he organized two black regiments and joined the Union army as a chaplain. After his term in the Senate, Revels served as the president of Alcorn Agricultural and Mechanical College in Western Mississippi.

Blanche Kelso Bruce was the first African American to serve a full term in the United States Senate. He represented Mississippi from 1875 to 1881. Bruce had been a slave who escaped at the beginning of the Civil War. During the war he taught school and studied at Oberlin College.

Joseph H. Rainey, also a former slave, was the first African American to serve in the United States House of Representatives. He represented South Carolina from 1870 to 1879. Afterward, Rainey became a special agent for the United States Treasury Department.

Robert Smalls was a member of the House of Representatives from 1875 to 1879 and again from 1881 to 1887. Smalls was a former slave who became a Civil War hero. During the war, he had been forced to serve as a wheelman on the Confederate steamship CSS *Planter*. One night when the captain was ashore, Smalls sailed the ship out of Charleston Harbor and turned it over to the Union navy. He then joined the Union navy as a ship's pilot.

Other African-American representatives in Congress included Benjamin S. Turner and James Rapier of Alabama, John Roy Lynch of Mississippi, Josiah T. Walls of Florida, Jefferson F. Long of Georgia, and Robert Brown Elliot, Richard Cain, Alonzo Ransier, and Robert C. DeLarge of South Carolina.

Pinckney Benton Stewart (P.B.S.) Pinchback had also been a slave. He raised a volunteer African-American company for the Union army during the war. In 1871, Pinchback was appointed lieutenant governor of

This lithograph depicts "Heroes of the Colored Race": Blanche Kelso Bruce, Frederick Douglass, and Hiram Rhoades Revels are surrounded by scenes of African American life as well as by portraits of other Americans—both black and white—who fought for civil rights.

Louisiana when Lieutenant Governor Oscar J. Dunn, another former slave, died. Pinchback was the acting governor of Louisiana for thirty-five days from December 1872 to January 1873. He was the first African-American governor in American history.

Chapter 6 ▶

An Incomplete Emancipation

For more than a century after the end of the Civil War, many white Southerners used any means possible to deny African Americans their rights. They were determined that blacks would remain second-class citizens.

Ku Klux Klan

During Reconstruction, some white Southerners formed secret groups to terrorize freedmen and keep them from voting. The most famous terror group was the Ku Klux Klan (KKK). Former Confederate officers, including General Nathan Bedford Forrest, founded the KKK in 1866 in Tennessee, and its influence spread throughout the South.

Klan members disguised themselves in white robes and pointed hoods, pretending to be the ghosts of dead Confederates. They rode on horseback by night and terrorized African Americans, carpetbaggers, scalawags, and anyone who supported blacks or voted for Republicans. Klansmen sent threatening messages and burned crosses as warnings. When that did not work, they resorted to more violent tactics. They beat freedmen and burned their houses. They also burned black schools and kidnapped African Americans and lynched them.

Victims of the KKK could do little to defend themselves. Many Southern whites, even those who did not belong to the KKK, agreed with the Klan's beliefs and

Formed shortly after the Civil War, the Ku Klux Klan infiltrated many areas of Southern government.

actions. In some places, there were law officers who were either Klansmen themselves or who supported Klan activities. When Republican sheriffs tried to stop the KKK, Klansmen threatened their families. If law officers did arrest KKK members, the Klan terrorized witnesses and jury members so that they could avoid conviction.

In 1870 and 1871, President Grant signed two Enforcement Acts. These laws, passed by Congress, made it a federal crime to interfere with voting rights, and they allowed the federal government to oversee elections. In 1871, Congress also passed the Ku Klux Klan Act, which authorized Union troops to track down and arrest Klansmen and others who terrorized African Americans.

President Grant sent federal soldiers into the South. Troops arrested several thousand KKK members. About

six hundred of them were convicted and served short prison sentences for their crimes.[1]

Jim Crow Laws

The Compromise of 1877 ended Reconstruction. Republican power in the South waned, and the Democratic party took hold. Southern states began passing laws that discriminated against African Americans and denied them equal rights with white Americans.

These laws were called Jim Crow laws after a popular song and dance that demeaned African Americans. Jim Crow laws banned African Americans from restaurants, theaters, hospitals, libraries, parks, and other public places. The laws forced African Americans to sit in blacks-only sections of trains, trolleys, and buses. Black children were not allowed to attend school with white children. Blacks could not drink from water fountains used by whites or swim in swimming pools that whites swam in. Blacks could not marry whites. They could not be buried in white cemeteries. Black prisoners even had to be kept in separate jails.

Laws forced voters to pass literacy tests and pay poll taxes. Anyone who could not pass the test or pay the tax could not cast a ballot. These laws kept African Americans, as well as many poor whites, from voting.

Racial prejudice was not limited to the South, however. African Americans faced discrimination all over the country. But the laws in Southern states were more severe. In the late 1800s, the United States Supreme Court ruled that these laws were not unconstitutional. The court ruled that segregation did not violate the Fourteenth Amendment. The Supreme Court also ruled that literacy voting tests did not discriminate against African Americans.

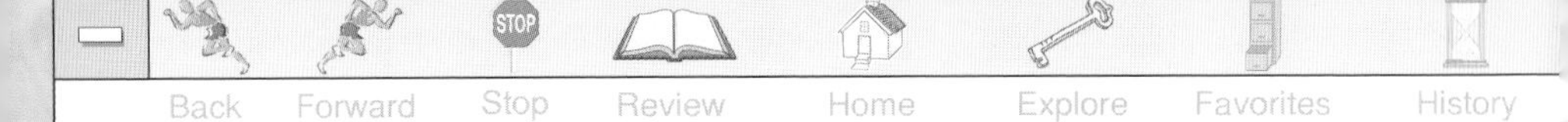

The Civil Rights Movement

African Americans struggled to gain equal rights. In 1909, on February 12, Abraham Lincoln's birthday, sixty African Americans and sympathetic whites formed the National Association for the Advancement of Colored People (NAACP). The NAACP fought for civil rights for African Americans. It crusaded against lynching and challenged unfair laws.

In 1954, NAACP lawyer Thurgood Marshall won a landmark case in the Supreme Court. In this case, *Brown* v. *Board of Education of Topeka, Kansas*, the Supreme Court ruled unanimously that school segregation was illegal. Still, Southern whites, backed by Southern governors, refused to allow black students into traditionally white schools. The federal government finally sent troops to enforce the ruling and to escort the African American students to school.

During the 1950s and 1960s, African Americans won more civil rights victories. In 1955, in Montgomery, Alabama, a black woman named Rosa Parks was arrested when she politely but firmly refused to give up her seat on a bus to a white man. In response, African Americans in Montgomery, led by the Reverend Martin Luther King, Jr., staged a bus boycott. They refused to ride Montgomery's buses for more than a year until a federal court declared that bus segregation was unconstitutional.

Civil rights activists staged peaceful marches and lunch-counter sit-ins all over the South to protest unfair laws. They boycotted businesses that discriminated against blacks and helped African Americans register to vote. Protesters were often attacked by policemen and arrested, but they continued to fight discrimination.

By standing up for their rights, African Americans risked their lives. After Reconstruction, the Ku Klux

Segregation depicted: A sign in a bus station in Rome, Georgia, in 1943, points the way to facilities for African Americans.

Klan's influence had faded although the Klan briefly resurfaced in the 1920s. Now, though, angry whites revived the secret society. The KKK countered African Americans' peaceful protests with violence. Klansmen threatened, beat, and killed African Americans and their supporters across the South. They often got away with their crimes because, just as during Reconstruction, many law enforcement officers and elected officials were either members of the Klan or agreed with the Klan's ideas.

In Birmingham, Alabama, Klansmen attacked black and white students who were riding a bus together as a form of protest. Klansmen bombed a Birmingham church, killing four African-American girls who were attending Sunday school. In 1963, a Klan member gunned down African-American civil rights leader Medgar Evers outside Evers' house in Jackson, Mississippi. In 1968, a white man, James Earl Ray, pleaded guilty to murdering Dr. Martin Luther King, Jr., in Memphis, Tennessee.

Today, laws protect the civil rights of African Americans, but nearly one hundred fifty years after the end of the Civil War, racism continues in the United States. The post–Civil War period of American history that is known as Reconstruction may have officially ended in 1877, but the divisions in America between North and South, black and white, still exist.

Chapter 1. The End of the War

1. Ulysses S. Grant, *Personal Memoirs of U. S. Grant* (New York: Penguin Books, 1999), p. 608.

Chapter 2. Reconstruction: The First Steps

1. William E. Gienapp, ed., *This Fiery Trial: The Speeches and Writings of Abraham Lincoln* (New York: Oxford University Press, 2002), p. 221.

2. Ibid.

3. "An Act to establish a Bureau for the Relief of Freedmen and Refugees," *The Freedmen's Bureau Act,* March 3, 1885, <http://www.history.umd.edu/Freedmen/fbact.htm> (December 14, 2003).

Chapter 3. President Johnson and the Radical Republicans

1. Andrew Johnson, quoted by Hans L. Trefousse, *Andrew Johnson, A Biography* (New York: W. W. Norton & Company, 1989), p. 131.

2. LeRoy P. Graf, ed., *The Papers of Andrew Johnson, Volume 7, 1864–1865* (Knoxville: The University of Tennessee Press, 1983), p. 583.

Chapter 4. Congressional Reconstruction

1. Brooks D. Simpson, *The Reconstruction Presidents* (Lawrence: University Press of Kansas, 1998), p. 88.

2. James M. McPherson, *Ordeal by Fire: The Civil War and Reconstruction* (Boston: McGraw-Hill, 2001), pp. 561–562.

3. "Constitution of the United States, Amendments 11–27," The National Archives Experience, <http://www.archives.gov/national_archives_experience/constitution_amendments_11-27.html> (December 14, 2003).

Chapter 6. An Incomplete Emancipation

1. James M. McPherson, *Ordeal by Fire: The Civil War and Reconstruction* (Boston: McGraw-Hill, 2001), p. 610.

Further Reading

Arnold, James R., and Roberta Wiener. *Lost Cause: The End of the Civil War, 1864–1865.* Minneapolis: Lerner Publications, 2002.

Collier, Christopher, and James Lincoln Collier. *Reconstruction and the Rise of Jim Crow.* New York: Marshall Cavendish, 2000.

Hakim, Joy. *Reconstruction and Reform.* New York: Oxford University Press, 1999.

_________. *War, Terrible War, 1860–1865.* New York: Oxford University Press, 1999.

Harper, Judith E. *Andrew Johnson, Our Seventeenth President.* Chanhassen, Minn.: Child's World, 2002.

Haskins, Jim. *The Geography of Hope: Black Exodus From the South After Reconstruction.* Brookfield, Conn.: Twenty-first Century Books, 1999.

McKissack, Patricia, and Fredrick McKissack. *Frederick Douglass: Leader Against Slavery.* Berkeley Heights, N.J.: 2002.

Stalcup, Brenda, ed. *Reconstruction: Opposing Viewpoints.* San Diego: Greenhaven Press, 1995.

Wormser, Richard. *The Dictionary of the Civil War and Reconstruction.* New York: Franklin Watts, 2000.

Ziff, Marsha. *Reconstruction Following the Civil War.* Springfield, N.J.: Enslow Publishers, Inc., 1999.

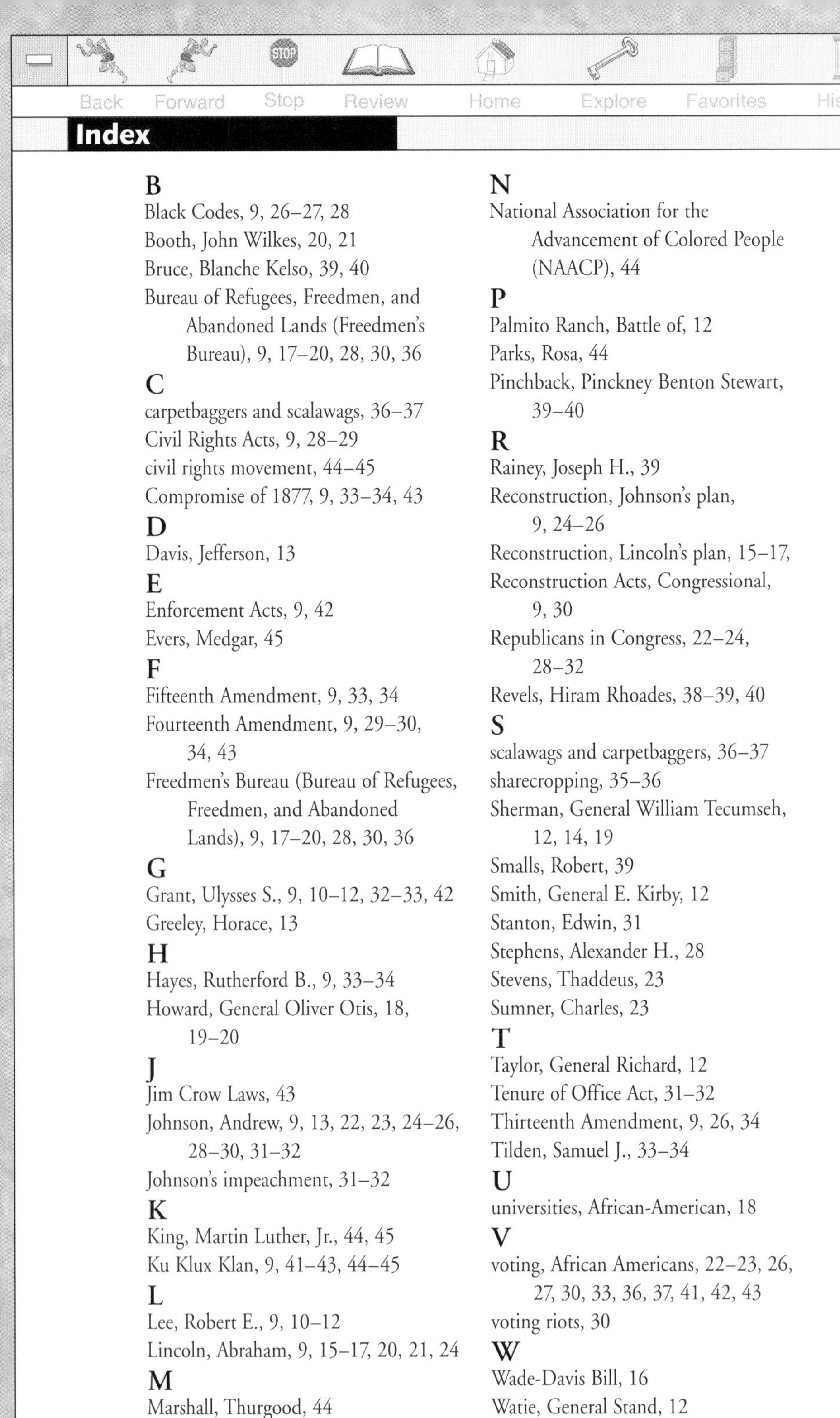

Index